Mason Jar Meals: 50 Creative, Delicious, and Easy to Make Lunch Recipes in a Jar

Disclaimer and Terms of Use: Effort has been made to ensure that the information in this book is accurate and complete, however, the author and the publisher do not warrant the accuracy of the information, text and graphics contained within the book due to the rapidly changing nature of science, research, known and unknown facts and internet. The Author and the publisher do not hold any responsibility for errors, omissions or contrary interpretation of the subject matter herein. This book is presented solely for motivational and informational purposes only.

Table of Contents

Eggplant special lunch 101

Jar full of veggies 103

Southwestern layered bell peppers 105

Soup Based Recipes

Velvet spinach soup

Serves: 2

Time: 10 minutes

Ingredients:

- 4 cups baby spinach, fresh
- ½ teaspoon olive oil
- 1 cup vegetable broth
- Salt and pepper – to taste
- 1/8 teaspoon curry powder
- 1 tablespoon onion, chopped
- ½ cup cooked great northern beans

Directions:

1. Heat oil in medium skillet; add onions and cook for 3-4 minutes.
2. Add spinach and cook until wilted; divide spinach-onion mixture between two standard Mason jars.
3. Divide remaining ingredients between the jars and apply blender base onto jar; attach the jar on the blender and process the soup until smooth.
4. Repeat with the second jar and serve immediately.

Nutrition Facts

Serving Size 232 g

Amount Per Serving

Calories 201	Calories from Fat 24

	% Daily Value*
Total Fat 2.6g	4%
Saturated Fat 0.6g	3%
Trans Fat 0.0g	
Cholesterol 0mg	0%
Sodium 436mg	18%
Potassium 1082mg	31%
Total Carbohydrates 31.7g	11%
Dietary Fiber 10.7g	43%
Sugars 1.8g	
Protein 14.2g	

Vitamin A 113%	•	Vitamin C 33%
Calcium 15%	•	Iron 25%

Nutrition Grade A

* Based on a 2000 calorie diet

Corn, basil buttermilk soup

Serves: 1

Time: 5 minutes

Ingredients:

- 1 ½ cups
- ½ cup corn kernels, fresh from the cob
- ¼ cup basil leaves
- 1 tablespoon diced onion
- ¼ cup peaches, diced
- ¼ tablespoon honey
- Salt and pepper to taste
- 2 teaspoons olive oil

Directions:

1. Heat oil in small skillet over medium-high heat; add diced onion and cook until tender.
2. Add corn and cook for 3 minutes.
3. Remove from the heat and when cooled transfer into Mason jar. Add remaining ingredients and apply the blender base on the Mason jar.
4. Process until smooth; microwave the soup on high for 60 seconds and serve after.

Nutrition Facts

Serving Size 518 g

Amount Per Serving

Calories 327   Calories from Fat 119

	% Daily Value*
Total Fat 13.2g	20%
Saturated Fat 3.4g	17%
Cholesterol 15mg	5%
Sodium 388mg	16%
Potassium 851mg	24%
Total Carbohydrates 42.0g	14%
Dietary Fiber 2.8g	11%
Sugars 28.3g	
Protein 14.9g	

Vitamin A 11%	•	Vitamin C 21%
Calcium 44%	•	Iron 14%

Nutrition Grade B+

* Based on a 2000 calorie diet

Cold avocado soup

Serves: 2

Time: 15 minutes

Ingredients:

- ½ cup yogurt
- ½ cup water
- ½ avocado, peeled and chopped
- 1 small cucumber, peeled, seeded and chopped
- 1 tablespoon dill weed, chopped finely
- ½ tablespoon chopped chives
- ½ teaspoon lemon juice
- Salt and pepper – to taste
- 2 pinches cayenne pepper

Directions:

1. Remove 2 tablespoons chopped cucumber to garnish.
2. Divide ingredients between two standard Mason jars.
3. Apply blender base on the jar and process until soup is smooth.
4. Repeat the process with the second jar.
5. Garnish soup with chopped cucumbers and pinch of cayenne pepper.
6. Chill in refrigerator for 1 hour before serving.

Nutrition Facts

Serving Size 325 g

Amount Per Serving

Calories 174   Calories from Fat 98

	% Daily Value*
Total Fat 10.8g	17%
Saturated Fat 2.7g	14%
Trans Fat 0.0g	
Cholesterol 4mg	1%
Sodium 54mg	2%
Potassium 669mg	19%
Total Carbohydrates 15.1g	5%
Dietary Fiber 4.4g	18%
Sugars 7.1g	
Protein 5.8g	

Vitamin A 10%	•	Vitamin C 20%
Calcium 17%	•	Iron 9%

Nutrition Grade A

* Based on a 2000 calorie diet

Gazpacho with watermelon

Serves: 2

Time: 15 minutes

Ingredients:

- 2 small pickling cucumbers, peeled and seeded
- 5 heirloom tomatoes, peeled and seeded
- ½ cup basil leaves, fresh
- 1 garlic clove, small
- 1 tablespoon red wine vinegar
- 1 tablespoon extra-virgin olive oil
- ½ hot chili pepper, seeded and chopped
- ¼ cup watermelon, cubed
- Salt and pepper – to taste

Directions:

1. Divide ingredients, except watermelon, between two standard Mason jars, equally.
2. Apply blender base on the Mason jar and process until smooth.
3. Repeat the process with the second jar.
4. Top the soup with watermelon cubes and serve.

Nutrition Facts

Serving Size 406 g

Amount Per Serving

Calories 153	Calories from Fat 74

	% Daily Value*
Total Fat 8.2g	13%
Saturated Fat 1.2g	6%
Trans Fat 0.0g	
Cholesterol 0mg	0%
Sodium 30mg	1%
Potassium 799mg	23%
Total Carbohydrates 20.8g	7%
Dietary Fiber 3.8g	15%
Sugars 4.8g	
Protein 3.4g	

Vitamin A 54%	•	Vitamin C 146%
Calcium 3%	•	Iron 10%

Nutrition Grade A

* Based on a 2000 calorie diet

Instant noodle soup

Serves: 1

Time: 15 minutes

Ingredients:

- 1 ½ oz. instant noodles
- 12 baby spinach leaves
- ½ cup shredded Napa cabbage
- ½ cup carrots, shredded
- 1/4th bouillon cube, crushed
- 1 tablespoon soy sauce, low sodium
- ½ teaspoon lime juice
- 1 ½ cups boiling water

Directions:

1. Break instant noodles in a bowl, until you get small pieces.
2. Place carrots, cabbage, soy sauce, lime juice, spinach, bouillon cube and noodles in a Mason jar.
3. Pour in boiling water and stir carefully; place aside for 12-13 minutes.
4. Serve after.

Nutrition Facts

Serving Size 624 g

Amount Per Serving

Calories 122	Calories from Fat 13

	% Daily Value*
Total Fat 1.4g	2%
Trans Fat 0.0g	
Cholesterol 12mg	4%
Sodium 1070mg	45%
Potassium 988mg	28%
Total Carbohydrates 22.4g	7%
Dietary Fiber 5.0g	20%
Sugars 4.1g	
Protein 7.3g	

Vitamin A 440%	•	Vitamin C 88%
Calcium 19%	•	Iron 24%

Nutrition Grade A

* Based on a 2000 calorie diet

Mexican soup

Serves: 2

Time: 10 minutes

Ingredients:

- 1 cup corn, canned
- 3 cups chicken stock, low sodium
- 6oz. salsa Verde
- 6oz. great northern beans, canned, rinsed and drained
- ½ cup chicken, cooked and shredded

Directions:

1. Divide ingredients between two standard Mason jars, equally.
2. Apply the lid and shake well.
3. Refrigerate for 3 hours and just before serving microwave on high for 120 seconds.
4. Serve and enjoy.

Nutrition Facts

Serving Size 648 g

Amount Per Serving

Calories 439 — Calories from Fat 32

	% Daily Value*
Total Fat 3.6g	6%
Saturated Fat 0.9g	5%
Cholesterol 27mg	9%
Sodium 1669mg	70%
Potassium 1446mg	41%
Total Carbohydrates 72.7g	24%
Dietary Fiber 19.3g	77%
Sugars 6.7g	
Protein 32.9g	

Vitamin A 8%	•	Vitamin C 33%
Calcium 19%	•	Iron 43%

Nutrition Grade A

* Based on a 2000 calorie diet

Curry soup

Serves: 1

Time: 10 minutes

Ingredients:

- 1 cup ramen noodles
- 1 teaspoon scallions, chopped finely
- ½ teaspoon curry
- ¼ cup carrots, chopped finely
- 1 ½ teaspoons chicken bouillon, crushed
- 2 tablespoons peas, frozen
- ¼ cup chicken breasts, cooked and shredded
- ¼ teaspoon sesame seeds
- Some boiling water

Directions:

1. Layer the bouillon cube or granules, carrots, scallions, peas, chicken, sesame seeds, curry powder and noodles in Mason jar.
2. Pour over boiling water, to cover the noodles and cover; place aside for 5 minutes.
3. Stir gently after and place aside for 5 minutes.
4. Serve and enjoy.

Nutrition Facts

Serving Size 245 g

Amount Per Serving

Calories 322	Calories from Fat 59

	% Daily Value*
Total Fat 6.5g	10%
Saturated Fat 1.5g	7%
Trans Fat 0.1g	
Cholesterol 78mg	26%
Sodium 101mg	4%
Potassium 304mg	9%
Total Carbohydrates 46.5g	16%
Dietary Fiber 4.0g	16%
Sugars 3.1g	
Protein 18.9g	

Vitamin A 96%	•	Vitamin C 16%
Calcium 5%	•	Iron 12%

Nutrition Grade B+

* Based on a 2000 calorie diet

Mushroom soup with pasta

Serves: 1

Time: 10 minutes

Ingredients:

- 1 cup cooked small pasta
- 1 teaspoon scallions, chopped
- 1 ½ teaspoons beef bouillon granules
- 1 teaspoon sesame seeds
- ¼ cup peas, frozen
- 1/3 cup shiitake mushrooms, sliced finely
- 1 teaspoon soy sauce
- Boiling water

Directions:

1. Layer the ingredients as follow in the jar; beef bouillon granules, mushrooms, peas, pasta, scallions, soy sauce and sesame seeds.
2. Pour over boiling water, to cover the pasta and stir it gently; place aside for 5 minutes.
3. Serve after, garnished with some chopped fresh parsley.

Nutrition Facts

Serving Size 255 g

Amount Per Serving

Calories 298	Calories from Fat 46

	% Daily Value*
Total Fat 5.1g	8%
Saturated Fat 0.9g	5%
Trans Fat 0.1g	
Cholesterol 46mg	15%
Sodium 468mg	19%
Potassium 238mg	7%
Total Carbohydrates 53.5g	18%
Dietary Fiber 5.2g	21%
Sugars 4.6g	
Protein 10.9g	

Vitamin A 7%	•	Vitamin C 25%
Calcium 6%	•	Iron 13%

Nutrition Grade A-

* Based on a 2000 calorie diet

Miso and vegetable soup in a jar

Serves: 1

Time: 15 minutes

Ingredients:

- 1 ½ cup boiling water
- 1 green onion, sliced thinly
- 1 handful spinach, torn
- 1 teaspoon miso paste
- ¼ cup shredded carrot
- ½ garlic clove, grated finely
- ½ red chili pepper, seeded and chopped
- 1 lime wedge, squeezed
- 1 teaspoon fresh grated ginger
- 1 small sweet red pepper, sliced into thin rounds
- 2 teaspoon soy sauce
- 2oz. tofu, diced

Directions:

1. Place ingredients in a Mason jar by order except boiling water and lime juice.
2. Give it a good stir and pour over boiling water.
3. Cover and place aside for 10 minutes.
4. Stir once again, season with lime juice and serve.

Nutrition Facts

Serving Size 549 g

Amount Per Serving

Calories 105	Calories from Fat 28

	% Daily Value*
Total Fat 3.1g	5%
Saturated Fat 0.6g	3%
Trans Fat 0.0g	
Cholesterol 0mg	0%
Sodium 854mg	36%
Potassium 443mg	13%
Total Carbohydrates 13.5g	4%
Dietary Fiber 3.8g	15%
Sugars 5.9g	
Protein 7.5g	

Vitamin A 143%	•	Vitamin C 166%
Calcium 16%	•	Iron 12%

Nutrition Grade A

* Based on a 2000 calorie diet

White gazpacho

Serves: 1

Time: 10 minutes

Ingredients:

- 1 ¼ cups water
- ¼ cup almonds, blanched
- 1 garlic clove, peeled and crushed
- 1 slice white rustic bread, crusts removed
- 2 teaspoons extra-virgin oil
- 1 teaspoon sherry vinegar
- Few halved white grapes – to garnish
- 1 teaspoon minced chives – to garnish
- Salt and white pepper – to taste

Directions:

1. Place bread in a bowl and pour in ¼ cup water. Place aside until bread is soaked, for 5 minutes.
2. Combine soaked bread, almonds, olive oil, sherry vinegar, garlic, water, salt and pepper in a Mason jar.
3. Apply the blender base on the jar and process the ingredients until smooth.
4. Top with halved grapes and minced chives before serving.

Nutrition Facts

Serving Size 323 g

Amount Per Serving

Calories 142   Calories from Fat 107

	% Daily Value*
Total Fat 11.9g	18%
Saturated Fat 0.9g	5%
Trans Fat 0.0g	
Cholesterol 0mg	0%
Sodium 10mg	0%
Potassium 189mg	5%
Total Carbohydrates 6.1g	2%
Dietary Fiber 3.0g	12%
Sugars 1.0g	
Protein 5.2g	

Vitamin A 0%	•	Vitamin C 2%
Calcium 8%	•	Iron 5%

Nutrition Grade A-

* Based on a 2000 calorie diet

Potato soup with bacon

Serves: 1

Time: 10 minutes

Ingredients:

- ¼ cup instant potato flakes
- 1 ¼ cups hot water
- ¼ teaspoon garlic powder
- 1/4th beef bouillon cube, crushed
- 1 tablespoon bacon bites
- 1 teaspoon dried chives
- 2 tablespoons powdered milk
- Salt and pepper – to taste

Directions:

1. Place all dry ingredients in a Mason jar.
2. Pour over hot water and apply the lid.
3. Shake well and place aside for 5 minutes.
4. Remove the lid and microwave for 90 seconds on high.
5. Stir once and microwave additional for 60 seconds on high.
6. Serve after, with pinch of smoked paprika.

Nutrition Facts

Serving Size 335 g

Amount Per Serving

Calories 135	Calories from Fat 10

	% Daily Value*
Total Fat 1.1g	2%
Trans Fat 0.0g	
Cholesterol 3mg	1%
Sodium 338mg	14%
Potassium 145mg	4%
Total Carbohydrates 21.0g	7%
Dietary Fiber 0.9g	4%
Sugars 8.6g	
Protein 10.2g	

Vitamin A 1%	•	Vitamin C 19%
Calcium 21%	•	Iron 3%

Nutrition Grade B

* Based on a 2000 calorie diet

Tortilla chicken soup

Serves: 1

Time: 15 minutes

Ingredients:

- 1 cup chicken broth
- ¼ avocado, diced small
- 1 corn tortilla, toasted and cut into strips
- 3oz. salsa
- ¼ cup corn kernels
- ½ cup chicken, grilled and shredded
- ¼ cup black beans
- ¾ tablespoon cilantro, fresh chopped

Directions:

1. Pour chicken broth and salsa in a standard Mason jar.
2. Microwave on high for 90 seconds.
3. Stir in corn, chicken and black beans.
4. Top the soup with tortillas, avocado and cilantro before serving.

Nutrition Facts

Serving Size 557 g

Amount Per Serving

Calories 518   Calories from Fat 135

	% Daily Value*
Total Fat 15.1g	23%
Saturated Fat 3.4g	17%
Trans Fat 0.0g	
Cholesterol 54mg	18%
Sodium 1335mg	56%
Potassium 1691mg	48%
Total Carbohydrates 59.0g	20%
Dietary Fiber 14.5g	58%
Sugars 6.0g	
Protein 40.3g	

Vitamin A 8%	•	Vitamin C 15%
Calcium 13%	•	Iron 31%

Nutrition Grade A

* Based on a 2000 calorie diet

Pie Based Recipes

Chicken pot pie

Serves: 6 pies

Time: 40 minutes

Ingredients:

- 2 tablespoons flour
- 3 tablespoons butter, divided
- 1 cup chicken, cooked and diced
- 1 cup chicken stock
- ½ cup peas, frozen
- 3 carrots, diced
- 2 cups milk
- ½ cup onion, diced
- Salt and pepper to taste
- Store bought dough for double pie crust

Directions:

1. Preheat oven to 425F.
2. Heat large frying pan over medium heat; add 2 teaspoons butter and when melted add carrots and cook for 3 minutes. Add onions and cook for 4-5 minutes, stirring occasionally. Place aside. In medium sauce pot melt remaining butter and when melted stir in flour.
3. Cook for 2-3 minutes, stirring constantly, until lightly brown. Whisk in milk and stock, bringing mixture to boil after each addition. Add peas and diced chicken and bring to simmer over medium heat. Simmer for 5-6 minutes.
   Meanwhile, roll out the dough to ¼-inch thick and line jars. Scoop the filling in the jars.
4. Roll out the remaining dough and cut out the top for the pie; prick hem few times with fork and place on top. Seal the edges. Place the pies onto baking sheet and bake for 15 minutes; cover the

pies with aluminum foil and bake for 15 minutes more. Remove from the oven and place aside to cool slightly before serving.

Nutrition Facts

Serving Size 207 g

Amount Per Serving

Calories 164	Calories from Fat 75
	% Daily Value*
Total Fat 8.3g	13%
Saturated Fat 4.9g	24%
Trans Fat 0.0g	
Cholesterol 40mg	13%
Sodium 243mg	10%
Potassium 238mg	7%
Total Carbohydrates 11.7g	4%
Dietary Fiber 1.6g	7%
Sugars 6.4g	
Protein 10.9g	

Vitamin A 108%	•	Vitamin C 12%
Calcium 12%	•	Iron 4%

Nutrition Grade B
* Based on a 2000 calorie diet

Lebanese pie in a jar

Serves: 6

Time: 30 minutes

Ingredients:

- 0.5lb. ground beef
- ½ tablespoon parsley, chopped
- ½ medium onion, chopped
- 1 tomato, diced
- ¼ teaspoon cinnamon
- ½ teaspoon salt
- ¼ teaspoon all spice
- ½ tablespoon sumac powder
- ¾ tablespoon ghee
- Small pinch cayenne pepper
- 2 tablespoons tahini
- 1 tablespoon pomegranate molasses
- 1 tablespoon lemon juice
- Pastry dough – for the pies
- ½ cup Greek yogurt

Directions:

1. Heat gee in medium skillet over medium-high heat; add onions and cook for 3 minutes.
2. Add the ground beef and cook until browned. Add the diced tomato and cook for 10 minutes.
3. Stir in the spices and cook for 1 minute: stir in the tahini paste and cook for 2 minutes.
4. Stir in pomegranate molasses and cook for 1 minute; stir in the lemon juice and remove from the heat to cool.
5. Meanwhile, roll out the dough to 1/8-inch thick. Line jars with dough and prick it few times with fork. Spoon the filling into jars.

Cut out the circles from the dough to make a top or the pie. Seal the edges and make a small "X" sin on top with sharp knife.

6. Transfer the jars onto baking sheet and bake for 15-18 minutes.
7. Remove the pies from the oven and place aside to cool slightly; top with Greek yogurt before serving.

Nutrition Facts

Serving Size 91 g

Amount Per Serving

Calories 145	Calories from Fat 62

	% Daily Value*
Total Fat 6.9g	11%
Saturated Fat 2.5g	12%
Trans Fat 0.0g	
Cholesterol 39mg	13%
Sodium 242mg	10%
Potassium 313mg	9%
Total Carbohydrates 6.4g	2%
Dietary Fiber 0.9g	3%
Sugars 4.0g	
Protein 13.7g	

Vitamin A 4%	•	Vitamin C 6%
Calcium 7%	•	Iron 43%

Nutrition Grade B+

* Based on a 2000 calorie diet

Shepherd's pie in a jar

Serves: 6

Time: 25 minutes

Ingredients:

- 0.5lb. ground beef
- 0.25lb. frozen peas
- 0.25lb. carrots, diced
- 4oz. V8 juice
- 1 onion, minced
- ½ cup grated parmesan
- 4 cups mashed potatoes
- ¼ cup all-purpose flour
- 2 teaspoons dried parsley
- 12oz. beef broth
- 1 teaspoon hot sauce, like tabasco
- Salta and pepper – to taste

Directions:

1. Heat non-stick skillet over medium high heat; add onions and beef. Cook until meat is browned.
2. Add peas and carrots and cook until all liquid is evaporated.
3. Add, hot sauce, salt and flour; stir until combined. Stir in V8 juice and beef broth; bring to boil.
4. Reduce heat and bring to simmer; simmer until mixture is slightly thickened for 15 minutes.
5. Preheat oven to 400F.
6. Combine mashed potatoes and parmesan in a bowl; spoon the mixture into piping bag, with plain nozzle and place aside.
7. Spoon the beef mixture into Mason jars and transfer them onto baking sheet; pipe out the mashed potatoes on top of beef and bake all for 15 minutes.
8. Serve after.

Nutrition Facts

Serving Size 338 g

Amount Per Serving

Calories 266   Calories from Fat 43

	% Daily Value*
Total Fat 4.8g	7%
Saturated Fat 1.8g	9%
Trans Fat 0.0g	
Cholesterol 37mg	12%
Sodium 632mg	26%
Potassium 874mg	25%
Total Carbohydrates 37.4g	12%
Dietary Fiber 2.2g	9%
Sugars 3.3g	
Protein 18.3g	

Vitamin A 76%	•	Vitamin C 19%
Calcium 6%	•	Iron 48%

Nutrition Grade A

* Based on a 2000 calorie diet

Lobster Pie

Serves: 2

Time: 40 minutes

Ingredients:

- 0.5lb lobster meat, cut into ¾-inch dices
- 1 tablespoon flour
- 1 ½ tablespoons butter
- 7oz. puff pastry
- ½ onion, minced
- 1 garlic clove, large, minced
- ¾ cup heavy cream
- 2 tablespoons brandy
- 1 egg, whisked
- Salt and pepper – to taste

Directions:

1. Melt butter in skillet over medium-high heat.
2. Add onion and garlic and cook for 5-6 minutes.
3. Add brandy and cook until reduced. Stir in cream and bring to boil; reduce heat and simmer until slightly thickened.
4. Stir in lobster meat and season to taste. Meanwhile, preheat oven to 425F.
5. Divide lobster meat between two Mason jars and place onto baking sheet. Roll the pastry dough on a slightly floured surface and cut out circles to cover Mason jars. Brush Mason jars edge with whisked egg and top with pastry.
6. Brush the pastry with egg and bake in preheated oven for 20 minutes.
7. Serve after.

Nutrition Facts

Serving Size 323 g

Amount Per Serving

Calories 939	Calories from Fat 597

	% Daily Value*
Total Fat 66.3g	102%
Saturated Fat 26.3g	132%
Cholesterol 332mg	111%
Sodium 909mg	38%
Potassium 438mg	13%
Total Carbohydrates 52.2g	17%
Dietary Fiber 2.2g	9%
Sugars 2.2g	
Protein 33.4g	

Vitamin A 21%	•	Vitamin C 4%
Calcium 17%	•	Iron 20%

Nutrition Grade C+

* Based on a 2000 calorie diet

Vegetable jar pie

Serves: 4

Time: 50 minutes

Ingredients:

For the crust:

- 1 cup whole wheat flour
- ¼ cup all-purpose flour
- 2 tablespoons cold butter, cut into cubes
- 3 tablespoons water
- ¼ teaspoon salt

For the filling:

- 1 tablespoon butter
- ½ cup onion, diced
- ½ cup celery, diced
- 1 ½ cups potatoes, diced
- 1 cup carrots, diced
- ½ cup peas, frozen
- 1 tablespoons chives, fresh, chopped
- ¼ cup flour
- 1 ½ cups chicken stock
- ½ tablespoon mustard

Directions:

1. Prepare the crust; combine flours and salt in a bowl. Work in butter dices and mix with hands.
2. Add water, gradually and mix until combined and dough forms.
3. Cover and place aside. Meanwhile, prepare the filling; melt the butter in sauce pot over medium heat.
4. Add veggies and cook until tender, for 5-6 minutes.

5. Add chicken stock and mustard; stir in flour. Bring mixture to boil and reduce heat to medium; simmer until slightly thickened.
6. Remove from the heat and place aside to cool slightly. Meanwhile, roll the dough to ¼-inch thick.
7. Cut out the tops for the pies using cookie cutter. Fill Mason jars with prepared veggie filling and top with the prepared dough.
8. Transfer the jars onto baking sheet and bake in preheated oven for 40 minutes.
9. Place aside to cool slightly before serving.

Nutrition Facts

Serving Size 292 g

Amount Per Serving

Calories 330	Calories from Fat 89
	% Daily Value*
Total Fat 9.9g	15%
Saturated Fat 5.6g	28%
Trans Fat 0.0g	
Cholesterol 23mg	8%
Sodium 530mg	22%
Potassium 485mg	14%
Total Carbohydrates 52.4g	17%
Dietary Fiber 5.0g	20%
Sugars 4.3g	
Protein 8.0g	

Vitamin A 102%	•	Vitamin C 36%
Calcium 5%	•	Iron 17%

Nutrition Grade B

* Based on a 2000 calorie diet

Beef jar pie

Serves: 4

Time: 40 minutes

Ingredients:

- 1 large russet potato, peeled and cut into dices
- 2 tablespoons vegetable oil
- 3 tablespoons butter
- 3 tablespoons plain flour
- ½ cup heavy cream, warmed
- 2 ½ cups beef stock, warm
- 2 tablespoons parsley, minced, fresh
- 2 cups frozen mixed vegetables, thawed
- 1 sheet puff pastry
- 1 egg, whisked
- Salt and pepper – to taste
- 1lb. beef, cut into ¾-inch cubes
- 1 small onion, diced

Directions:

1. Preheat oven to 375F.
2. Place the potatoes in sauce pot and cover with water; add some salt and bring to boil over medium-high heat.
3. Reduce heat and simmer until potatoes are fork tender, for 5-6 minutes. Drain and place aside.
4. Heat vegetable oil in large skillet; add beef and cook until browned.
5. Transfer beef with slotted spoon in a bowl.
6. Place onion in same skillet where the beef cooked; cook the onions for 5-6 minutes or until tender. Remove and place on top of beef.
7. Melt butter in the same skillet and when melted stir in the flour; cook flour until slightly browned, mixing constantly.

8. Stir in beef stock and heavy cream; bring to gentle boil. Reduce heat and simmer mixture until slightly thickened.
9. Stir in the beef, thawed veggies, potatoes and onion. Add parsley and season to taste. Sime for 15 minutes.
10. Divide mixture between four Mason jars. Roll the puff pastry on slightly floured surface and cut out the circles with cookie cutter that fit on the Mason jar.
11. Brush pastry with whisked egg and transfer the Mason jars onto baking sheet. Bake pies for 30 minutes.
12. Let them cool slightly before serving.

Nutrition Facts

Serving Size 423 g

Amount Per Serving	
Calories 513	Calories from Fat 267

	% Daily Value*
Total Fat 29.7g	46%
Saturated Fat 13.5g	67%
Cholesterol 186mg	62%
Sodium 680mg	28%
Potassium 762mg	22%
Total Carbohydrates 18.7g	6%
Dietary Fiber 4.6g	18%
Sugars 3.7g	
Protein 41.3g	

Vitamin A 92%	•	Vitamin C 11%
Calcium 6%	•	Iron 128%

Nutrition Grade B
* Based on a 2000 calorie diet

Chicken and butternut squash pie

Serves: 4

Time: 60 minutes

Ingredients:

- ¼ cup all-purpose flour
- 1 ½ cups butternut squash, cut into ½-inch pieces
- 1 ½ cups shredded chicken
- 1 small bunch kale, stems removed, leaves chopped
- ¼ cup oil
- 1 onion, chopped
- 3 cups chicken broth
- 1 tablespoon sage, fresh, chopped
- Salt and pepper – to taste
- 1 egg, whisked

Directions:

1. Preheat oven to 425F.
2. Heat oil in large skillet; add onion and cook until tender, for 5-6 minutes over medium-high heat.
3. Add chopped kale and cook until wilted, for 4-5 minutes. Sprinkle with flour and cook, stirring constantly for 4 minutes.
4. Stir in broth, ½ cup at the time; add squash and bring to boil.
5. Reduce heat and simmer until squash is tender and broth is thickened, for 8-10 minutes.
6. Add chicken to the skillet and season all with salt and pepper to taste.
7. Transfer filling in wide mouth Mason jar. Roll the pastry and cut out the tops that will perfectly fit on the Mason jars.
8. Brush pastry with egg and transfer jars onto baking sheet. Bake for 15 minutes at 425F; reduce heat and bake for 15 minutes more at 375F.
9. Let cool for 10 minutes before serving.

Nutrition Facts

Serving Size 345 g

Amount Per Serving

Calories 309	Calories from Fat 158
	% Daily Value*
Total Fat 17.6g	27%
Saturated Fat 2.9g	15%
Trans Fat 0.0g	
Cholesterol 81mg	27%
Sodium 624mg	26%
Potassium 506mg	14%
Total Carbohydrates 15.7g	5%
Dietary Fiber 2.1g	8%
Sugars 3.0g	
Protein 21.9g	

Vitamin A 113%	•	Vitamin C 22%
Calcium 6%	•	Iron 11%

Nutrition Grade B

* Based on a 2000 calorie diet

Turkey pie in jar

Serves: 4

Time: 50 minutes

Ingredients:

- 3 cups turkey meat, cooked and shredded
- ½ cup milk
- 1 ¾ cup chicken broth
- ¼ cup butter, unsalted
- 2 garlic cloves, mined
- 1/3 cup plain flour
- 4 cups vegetable mix, fresh, chopped
- 1 small onion, chopped
- 1 egg, whisked
- Pie crust dough

Directions:

1. Preheat oven to 425F.
2. Roll the dough to ¼-inch thick and line jars with dough, bottom and sides.
3. Cut the circles from the remaining dough large enough to cover the tops of the jars and prick with fork. Meth the butter in skillet over medium-high heat; add onions and vegetables and cook until tender. Stir in flour and season with salt and pepper to taste. Gradually stir in milk and chicken broth. Continue stirring until smooth and thick. Fold in turkey meat.
4. Fill each jar with prepared mixture and top with dough. Transfer onto baking sheet and bake for 15 minutes; cover with aluminum foil and bake for 15 minutes more.
5. Let the pies cool for 10 minutes before serving.

Nutrition Facts

Serving Size 538 g

Amount Per Serving

Calories 455	Calories from Fat 173

	% Daily Value*
Total Fat 19.2g	30%
Saturated Fat 9.9g	50%
Trans Fat 0.0g	
Cholesterol 153mg	51%
Sodium 1100mg	46%
Potassium 482mg	14%
Total Carbohydrates 28.1g	9%
Dietary Fiber 4.6g	18%
Sugars 6.4g	
Protein 38.7g	

Vitamin A 228%	•	Vitamin C 23%
Calcium 14%	•	Iron 72%

Nutrition Grade B

* Based on a 2000 calorie diet

Pasta Based recipes

Pasta with Pepperoni

Serves: 6

Time: 40 minutes

Ingredients:

- 1 ½ cups broken spaghetti, uncooked
- ½ cup grated parmesan cheese
- 3 eggs
- 1lb. ricotta
- 3oz. sliced pepperoni
- Salt and pepper – to taste

Directions:

1. Preheat oven to 350F.
2. Cook pasta cording to package instructions until al dente. Drain and stir in ricotta and pepperoni.
3. Meanwhile, whisk the eggs with black pepper. Fold into pasta.
4. Divide pasta between six Mason jars; pour over eggs and top with peperoni.
5. Transfer jars onto baking sheet and bake for 30 minutes.
6. Cool slightly before serving.

Nutrition Facts

Serving Size 212 g

Amount Per Serving

Calories 577   Calories from Fat 143

	% Daily Value*
Total Fat 15.9g	24%
Saturated Fat 6.8g	34%
Trans Fat 0.2g	
Cholesterol 120mg	40%
Sodium 366mg	15%
Potassium 387mg	11%
Total Carbohydrates 78.7g	26%
Dietary Fiber 3.2g	13%
Sugars 3.1g	
Protein 27.6g	

Vitamin A 8%	•	Vitamin C 0%
Calcium 24%	•	Iron 24%

Nutrition Grade B+

* Based on a 2000 calorie diet

Pasta with tomato sauce

Serves: 4

Time: 20 minutes

Ingredients:

- 8oz. uncooked pasta
- 8oz. can crushed tomatoes
- ½ teaspoon dried oregano
- 1 teaspoon rosemary fresh
- ¼ teaspoon chili flakes
- 1 tablespoon grated parmesan
- 3 tablespoon cottage cheese
- 2 tablespoons ricotta cheese
- 1 tablespoon mozzarella cheese
- 1 tablespoon parmesan cheese, grated
- Salt and pepper – to taste

Directions:

1. Cook pasta in pot with salted boiling water until al dente; drain.
2. Meanwhile, combine together cottage cheese, ricotta and mozzarella cheese. Stir cheese mixture into pasta and transfer the content into Mason jars.
3. Combine crushed tomatoes with rosemary, chili flakes, oregano and Parmesan in a bowl.
4. Pour the tomato mix over pasta, moving pasta so the sauce reaches the bottom of a jar.
5. Preheat oven to 350F and transfer jars onto baking sheet; bake the pasta in oven for 15-18 minutes; serve cooled slightly.

Nutrition Facts

Serving Size 249 g

Amount Per Serving

Calories 172	Calories from Fat 21
	% Daily Value*
Total Fat 2.4g	4%
Saturated Fat 0.9g	4%
Trans Fat 0.0g	
Cholesterol 25mg	8%
Sodium 335mg	14%
Potassium 661mg	19%
Total Carbohydrates 31.1g	10%
Dietary Fiber 3.9g	16%
Protein 9.4g	

Vitamin A 30%	•	Vitamin C 31%
Calcium 12%	•	Iron 21%

Nutrition Grade A

* Based on a 2000 calorie diet

Mac and cheese

Serves: 4

Time: 10 minutes

Ingredients:

- 8oz. elbow pasta, uncooked
- ½ cup heavy cream
- 4 tablespoons cream cheese
- 8oz. smoky cheddar cheese, shredded
- 1 tablespoon spicy mustard
- Salt and pepper – to taste
- 1 tablespoon water

Directions:

1. Cook pasta according to package directions in pot of salted boiling water, until al dente.
2. Meanwhile, whisk heavy cream, cream cheese, water and spicy mustard.

3. When pasta is cooked, drain it and stir in cream cheese mixture.
4. Transfer pasta into Mason jars and top with shredded cheddar cheese.
5. Microwave pasta for 90 seconds; apply the lid, shake well and microwave again for 90 seconds, without the lid.
6. Serve after.

Nutrition Facts

Serving Size 142 g

Amount Per Serving

Calories 504	Calories from Fat 259

	% Daily Value*
Total Fat 28.8g	44%
Saturated Fat 17.6g	88%
Cholesterol 91mg	30%
Sodium 397mg	17%
Potassium 79mg	2%
Total Carbohydrates 41.2g	14%
Dietary Fiber 6.0g	24%
Protein 24.1g	

Vitamin A 18%	•	Vitamin C 0%
Calcium 45%	•	Iron 18%

Nutrition Grade C+

* Based on a 2000 calorie diet

Baked pasta with pesto and zucchinis

Serves: 4

Time: 35 minutes

Ingredients:

- 10oz. pasta
- 8oz. zucchinis, grated
- 2oz. breadcrumbs
- 5oz. basil pesto
- 1 ¾ cups crème fraiche
- Salt and pepper – to taste

Directions:

1. Cook pasta according to package directions until al dente. Reserve some of the cooking liquid.
2. Meanwhile, mix pesto, crème fraiche and zucchinis together.
3. Add pasta and stir well; gradually add pasta cooking liquid and stir until you get sauce consistency.
4. Transfer pasta into Mason jars; top with breadcrumbs and slightly drizzle with olive oil.
5. Bake the pasts in preheated oven for 20 minutes. Serve when cooled slightly.

Nutrition Facts

Serving Size 177 g

Amount Per Serving

Calories 277	Calories from Fat 24

	% Daily Value*
Total Fat 2.7g	4%
Cholesterol 52mg	17%
Sodium 129mg	5%
Potassium 408mg	12%
Total Carbohydrates 51.8g	17%
Dietary Fiber 1.8g	7%
Sugars 2.0g	
Protein 11.7g	

Vitamin A 40%	•	Vitamin C 27%
Calcium 11%	•	Iron 24%

Nutrition Grade A

* Based on a 2000 calorie diet

Pasta with mushrooms and tuna

Serves: 4

Time: 25 minutes

Ingredients:

- 10oz. spiral pasta
- ¼ cup parsley, chopped
- 1 ½ cups thickened cream
- 7oz. mushrooms, sliced
- 10oz. can tuna, drained, 1 tablespoon oil reserved
- 1 cup grated cheese, like parmesan
- 2 teaspoons wholegrain mustard
- Salt and pepper – to taste

Directions:

1. Cook pasta according to package directions, until al dente.
2. Meanwhile, heat reserved tuna oil in medium skillet over medium-high heat; add mushrooms and cook until tender.
3. Add cream and simmer for 2-3 minutes.
4. When pasta is cooked, drain it and stir in mushrooms, along with tuna, parsley and mustard.
5. Season with salt and pepper to taste and transfer into four Mason jars. Top pasta with cheese.
6. Place the jars onto baking sheet and bake in preheated oven for 15 minutes.
7. Serve after.

Nutrition Facts

Serving Size 223 g

Amount Per Serving

Calories 533	Calories from Fat 174

	% Daily Value*
Total Fat 19.3g	30%
Saturated Fat 7.3g	37%
Cholesterol 30mg	10%
Sodium 854mg	36%
Potassium 206mg	6%
Total Carbohydrates 53.5g	18%
Dietary Fiber 3.1g	12%
Sugars 3.5g	
Protein 34.4g	

Vitamin A 12%	•	Vitamin C 11%
Calcium 21%	•	Iron 23%

Nutrition Grade C+

* Based on a 2000 calorie diet

Cheesy pasta with spinach

Serves: 4

Time: 30 minutes

Ingredients:

- 10oz. pasta
- 8oz. frozen spinach, thawed
- 1 cup frozen peas, thawed
- 3 eggs
- 4oz. sliced ham, coarsely chopped
- ¾ cup thickened cream
- 1 cup cheese, grated
- ½ cup can corn kernels, drained

Directions:

1. Preheat oven to 350F.
2. Cook pasta according to package directions until al dente.
3. Meanwhile, squeeze spinach to remove excess liquid; place in a bowl and combine with cooked pasta, corns, peas, ham and cheese.
4. Fill four Mason jars with pasta mix and transfer onto baking sheet.
5. Whisk eggs with thickened cream and pour over pasta.
6. Bake pasta for 20 minutes; serve warm.

Nutrition Facts

Serving Size 257 g

Amount Per Serving

Calories 456	Calories from Fat 153

	% Daily Value*
Total Fat 17.0g	26%
Saturated Fat 8.1g	41%
Trans Fat 0.0g	
Cholesterol 220mg	73%
Sodium 683mg	28%
Potassium 641mg	18%
Total Carbohydrates 48.3g	16%
Dietary Fiber 3.8g	15%
Sugars 2.5g	
Protein 27.6g	

Vitamin A 133%	•	Vitamin C 35%
Calcium 30%	•	Iron 31%

Nutrition Grade A-

* Based on a 2000 calorie diet

Dairy free Mac and cheese

Serves: 4

Time: 30 minutes

Ingredients:

- 8oz. pasta
- 2 cups soy milk, reduced
- 4 green onion, sliced thinly
- 3oz. soy cheese, grated
- 3oz. ham, chopped
- 2 tablespoons all-purpose flour
- 6oz. broccoli, cut into small florets
- 1 tablespoon vegetable shortening
- Salt and pepper – to taste

Directions:

1. Preheat oven to 350F.
2. Cook pasta in large pot of salted boiling water, until al dente, adding broccoli florets in 2-3 last minutes of cooking.
3. Drain well and place in colander.
4. Melt vegetable shortening in sauce pot over medium heat: stir in flour and cook until slightly browned, stirring constantly.
5. Fold in milk, gradually and bring to boil; cook for 5 minutes, whisking, until slightly thick.
6. Remove from the heat and stir in grated cheese; season to taste.
7. Combine pasta and broccoli with ham and onions; spoon into four wide mouth Mason jars and pour over prepared sauce; bake in preheated oven for 20 minutes or until golden.
8. Serve while still hot.

Nutrition Facts

Serving Size 340 g

Amount Per Serving

Calories 378	Calories from Fat 112

	% Daily Value*
Total Fat 12.4g	19%
Saturated Fat 3.5g	18%
Trans Fat 0.0g	
Cholesterol 54mg	18%
Sodium 588mg	25%
Potassium 487mg	14%
Total Carbohydrates 47.9g	16%
Dietary Fiber 2.6g	11%
Sugars 6.0g	
Protein 17.3g	

Vitamin A 9%	•	Vitamin C 69%
Calcium 8%	•	Iron 20%

Nutrition Grade B

* Based on a 2000 calorie diet

Angel hair pasta with garlic

Serves: 6

Time: 10 minutes

Ingredients:

- 14oz. angel hair pasta
- ½ cup breadcrumbs
- ½ cup olive oil
- 6 garlic cloves, sliced thinly
- Juice and zest of 1 lemon
- 1 ½ small red chilies seeded and chopped
- Salt –to taste

Directions:

1. Fill six Mason jars with boiling water; add in angel hair pasta and microwave on high for 3 minutes.
2. Remove the pasta and stir gently; microwave for 2 minutes more.
3. Meanwhile, prepare the sauce; heat 1 tablespoon olive oil in large skillet; add breadcrumbs and cook over medium heat for 2 minutes; remove and wipe the pan.
4. Heat remaining oil and when sizzling add garlic and chilies. Cook for 2 minutes or until garlic is light golden.
5. Season with salt to taste and add lemon juice and zest; remove from the heat.
6. Top pasta with breadcrumb mixture and garlic sauce; apply the lid and shake well.
7. Serve after.

Nutrition Facts

Serving Size 106 g

Amount Per Serving

Calories 377   Calories from Fat 169

	% Daily Value*
Total Fat 18.8g	29%
Saturated Fat 2.7g	14%
Cholesterol 48mg	16%
Sodium 84mg	4%
Potassium 163mg	5%
Total Carbohydrates 44.5g	15%
Dietary Fiber 0.6g	3%
Sugars 0.8g	
Protein 9.0g	

Vitamin A 1%	•	Vitamin C 13%
Calcium 3%	•	Iron 15%

Nutrition Grade B-

* Based on a 2000 calorie diet

Lasagna jars

Serves: 4

Time: 45 minutes

Ingredients:

- 1lb. beef, ground
- 2 garlic cloves, minced
- 4oz. tomato paste
- 3oz. can diced tomatoes
- 2 tablespoons basil, fresh, chopped
- 1 cup Parmesan, shredded
- 10oz. ricotta
- 1/3 cup mozzarella
- 1 tablespoon olive oil
- Salt and pepper – to taste
- 2 sheets no-boil lasagna noodles, broken into pieces

Directions:

1. Preheat oven to 370F.
2. Heat ½ tablespoon olive oil in large skillet; add 1 garlic clove and cook for 1 minute. Add ground beef and cook until browned. Place aside.
3. In sauce pan heat remaining olive oil and add garlic; cook until fragrant for 1 minute.
4. Add diced tomatoes, along with tomato paste, basil and 1 ½ tablespoons parmesan.
5. Bring to boil and reduce heat; simmer for 3-4 minutes and remove from the heat.
6. In a bowl combine mozzarella and ricotta and half of the remaining parmesan.
7. Combine tomato sauce and ground beef; season to taste.
8. Layer lasagna in four mason jars in the following order; turkey with pasta sauce, lasagna noodles, cheese filling and sprinkle of

remaining parmesan cheese. Place the jars onto baking sheet and bake in preheated oven for 40 minutes, covered with foil. Allow to cool for 5 minutes before serving.

Nutrition Facts

Serving Size 250 g

Amount Per Serving

Calories 395	Calories from Fat 162
	% Daily Value*
Total Fat 18.0g	28%
Saturated Fat 7.7g	38%
Trans Fat 0.0g	
Cholesterol 128mg	43%
Sodium 293mg	12%
Potassium 843mg	24%
Total Carbohydrates 11.0g	4%
Dietary Fiber 1.6g	6%
Sugars 4.4g	
Protein 46.7g	

Vitamin A 19%	•	Vitamin C 14%
Calcium 28%	•	Iron 126%

Nutrition Grade B+

* Based on a 2000 calorie diet

Pasta salad

Serves: 4

Time: 15 minutes

Ingredients:

- 2 cups pasta, cooked
- ¾ quart grape tomatoes
- 8 cups baby spinach
- 8oz. fresh mozzarella, torn into pieces
- 8 tablespoons balsamic vinegar

Directions:

1. Divide ingredients equally between four Mason jars.
2. Start with balsamic vinegar, tomatoes, mozzarella, pasta and ending with spinach.
3. Just before use, place lid on jar and shake well. Serve after.

Nutrition Facts

Serving Size 346 g

Amount Per Serving

Calories 391	Calories from Fat 109

	% Daily Value*
Total Fat 12.1g	19%
Saturated Fat 6.4g	32%
Trans Fat 0.0g	
Cholesterol 77mg	26%
Sodium 416mg	17%
Potassium 791mg	23%
Total Carbohydrates 44.8g	15%
Dietary Fiber 2.9g	12%
Sugars 3.9g	
Protein 26.4g	

Vitamin A 144%	•	Vitamin C 59%	
Calcium 49%	•	Iron 23%	

Nutrition Grade A-

* Based on a 2000 calorie diet

Macaroni ham pie

Serves: 6

Time: 60 minutes

Ingredients:

- 3 cups shredded cheddar cheese
- 1 cup uncooked macaroni, like elbow
- 2 eggs
- 2 ¼ cups milk
- ½ cup flour
- 1 teaspoon baking powder
- ¼ teaspoon salt
- 1 cup ham, cooked and diced

Directions:

1. Heat oven to 400FD and slightly grease six Mason jars.
2. In a bowl combine 2 cups cheese and uncooked macaroni. Add ham and divide evenly between the jars.
3. Whisk eggs with milk; sift over flour, salt and baking powder. Mix well until smooth.
4. Pour over macaroni, dividing evenly.
5. Bake for 40 minutes; sprinkle the jar content with remaining cheese and bake for 1-2 minutes more. Serve after, garnished with some chopped fresh parsley.

Nutrition Facts

Serving Size 211 g

Amount Per Serving

Calories 422	Calories from Fat 219

	% Daily Value*
Total Fat 24.3g	37%
Saturated Fat 14.2g	71%
Trans Fat 0.0g	
Cholesterol 134mg	45%
Sodium 807mg	34%
Potassium 318mg	9%
Total Carbohydrates 25.0g	8%
Dietary Fiber 1.0g	4%
Sugars 4.9g	
Protein 25.6g	

Vitamin A 13%	•	Vitamin C 2%
Calcium 57%	•	Iron 11%

Nutrition Grade B-

* Based on a 2000 calorie diet

Chicken Alfredo Pasta Bake

Serves: 4

Time: 40 minutes

Ingredients:

- 8oz. penne pasta
- 4oz. sour cream
- 1 cup Alfredo sauce
- ½ tablespoon parsley, fresh, chopped
- 7oz. ricotta cheese
- 1 cup chicken, grilled and cubed
- 1 egg, beaten
- 1 cup mozzarella cheese, shredded
- Salt and pepper – to taste

Directions:

1. Cook the pasta according to package directions, until al dente.
2. Drain pasta and mix with Alfredo sauce in a bowl; add chicken and sour cream.
3. In separate bowl combine ricotta, eggs and parmesan; add parsley and mix until combined thoroughly. Stir in the pasta and mix until coated.
4. Transfer pasta in Mason jars and preheat oven to 350F.
5. Top pasta with mozzarella cheese and place onto baking sheet; bake pasta for 30 minutes.
6. You can additionally broil pasta for 2-3 minutes to get a nice brown crust; serve after.

Nutrition Facts

Serving Size 239 g

Amount Per Serving

Calories 565	Calories from Fat 214

	% Daily Value*
Total Fat 23.7g	37%
Saturated Fat 13.3g	66%
Trans Fat 0.0g	
Cholesterol 163mg	54%
Sodium 1760mg	73%
Potassium 287mg	8%
Total Carbohydrates 50.1g	17%
Protein 36.9g	

Vitamin A 14%	•	Vitamin C 2%
Calcium 39%	•	Iron 15%

Nutrition Grade D

* Based on a 2000 calorie diet

Pizza pasta salad

Serves: 4

Time: 15 minutes

Ingredients:

- 2 cups cooked pasta, tri-color
- ½ cup sliced pepperoni
- 3oz. pitted black olives
- ½ green bell pepper, chopped
- 4 tablespoons parmesan cheese, shredded
- 4oz. cherry tomatoes, halved
- 4oz. mozzarella cheese, cubed
- ¼ cup Italian salad dressing

Directions:

1. Cook pasta according to package directions, until al dente.
2. Drain well and divide between four Mason jars.
3. Add mozzarella and tomatoes and stir; add olives and stir; add pepperoni and stir to combine.
4. Pour over Italian dressing and top with chopped bell pepper.
5. Apply lid and shake to coat the pasta with sauce; serve after.

Nutrition Facts

Serving Size 209 g

Amount Per Serving

Calories 506	Calories from Fat 241

	% Daily Value*
Total Fat 26.8g	41%
Saturated Fat 9.7g	49%
Trans Fat 0.4g	
Cholesterol 107mg	36%
Sodium 910mg	38%
Potassium 292mg	8%
Total Carbohydrates 41.4g	14%
Dietary Fiber 1.3g	5%
Sugars 2.6g	
Protein 25.7g	

Vitamin A 22%	•	Vitamin C 39%
Calcium 35%	•	Iron 19%

Nutrition Grade B-

* Based on a 2000 calorie diet

Pasta with sausage and spinach

Serves: 4

Time: 40 minutes

Ingredients:

- 2 cups marinara sauce
- ½ teaspoon olive oil
- 4oz. ricotta
- 4oz. mozzarella
- 6oz. Italian sausage, uncooked and removed from casing
- 6oz. rigatoni pasta
- 5oz. frozen spinach, thawed
- 1 garlic clove, finely chopped
- ¼ cup Pecorino Romano, grated
- Salt and pepper – to taste

Directions:

1. Preheat oven to 375F.
2. Cook pasta until al dente, according to package instructions.
3. In a medium bowl combine ricotta, 2 tablespoons Pecorino Romano, and half of the mozzarella cheese. Heat oil in medium skillet and add garlic; cook until fragrant. Add sausage and cook until browned, braking any lumps.
4. Add spinach, season to taste cook for 1 minutes. Pour in marinara sauce and cook on low for 2-3 minutes. Place half of the pasta in Mason jars; top with half of meat sauce. Spoon ricotta mixture evenly and cover with remaining pasta and meat sauce. Top meat sauce with mozzarella and reserved Pecorino Romano. Cover with foil and bake for 20 minutes. Remove foil and bake further for 5-6 minutes; serve after, while still hot.

Nutrition Facts

Serving Size 304 g

Amount Per Serving

Calories 512	Calories from Fat 219

	% Daily Value*
Total Fat 24.3g	37%
Saturated Fat 9.4g	47%
Trans Fat 0.1g	
Cholesterol 93mg	31%
Sodium 1077mg	45%
Potassium 897mg	26%
Total Carbohydrates 44.0g	15%
Dietary Fiber 3.7g	15%
Sugars 11.2g	
Protein 27.9g	

Vitamin A 64%	•	Vitamin C 9%
Calcium 35%	•	Iron 19%

Nutrition Grade B-

* Based on a 2000 calorie diet

Other meals

Corn dogs

Serves: 6

Time: 25 minutes

Ingredients:

- 3 eggs
- 1 ½ cups self-rising corn meal
- ¼ cup sugar
- ¾ cup milk
- 2 tablespoons oil
- ¼ cup sour cream
- 3 hot dogs, cut in half
- 1/3 cup cheese, grated – by your choice

Directions:

1. Preheat oven to 375F.
2. Combine the eggs, flour, sugar, milk, oil and cream in food processor; pulse until you have smooth mixture.
3. Spoon the batter into six Mason jars and place the hot dog in the middle of the batter.
4. Bake for 20 minutes in preheated oven. Top the corn dogs with grated cheese and broil for 2 minutes.
5. Serve after.

Nutrition Facts

Serving Size 115 g

Amount Per Serving

Calories 270	Calories from Fat 109

	% Daily Value*
Total Fat 12.1g	19%
Saturated Fat 4.2g	21%
Trans Fat 0.0g	
Cholesterol 95mg	32%
Sodium 543mg	23%
Potassium 67mg	2%
Total Carbohydrates 35.8g	12%
Dietary Fiber 1.3g	5%
Sugars 9.9g	
Protein 8.3g	

Vitamin A 5%	•	Vitamin C 0%
Calcium 18%	•	Iron 8%

Nutrition Grade C+

* Based on a 2000 calorie diet

Mason jar Cordon bleu

Serves: 4

Time: 50 minutes

Ingredients:

- 5 slices Swiss cheese
- 5 slices smoked turkey ham
- 1lb. chicken fillets
- ½ tablespoon parsley flakes
- Salt and pepper – to taste
- ¼ cup butter, melted
- ¾ cup breadcrumbs

Directions:

1. Place chicken fillets onto clean foil, so they slightly overlap and cover with another piece of foil.
2. Pound meat with meat tenderizer until you have kind of large sheet; season with salt and pepper.
3. Cover chicken with ham followed with cheese and using plastic wrap and working from the farthest side roll the meat towards you.
4. Cut chicken in four equal slices and place in wide mouth Mason jars.
5. Melt butter and season with salt and pepper; stir in parsley flakes and breadcrumbs. Divide the breadcrumbs over chicken and transfer jars onto baking sheet. Bake in preheated oven for 20 minutes, uncovered. Cover the cordon bleu with foil and continue baking for 20 minutes more.
6. Serve while still hot.

Nutrition Facts

Serving Size 194 g

Amount Per Serving

Calories 543	Calories from Fat 282

	% Daily Value*
Total Fat 31.3g	48%
Saturated Fat 16.2g	81%
Cholesterol 170mg	57%
Sodium 520mg	22%
Potassium 348mg	10%
Total Carbohydrates 16.8g	6%
Dietary Fiber 0.9g	4%
Sugars 2.0g	
Protein 46.6g	

Vitamin A 15%	•	Vitamin C 1%
Calcium 33%	•	Iron 14%

Nutrition Grade C+

* Based on a 2000 calorie diet

Quiche in a jar

Serves: 4

Time: 45 minutes

Ingredients:

- 6 eggs
- ½ teaspoon salt
- ½ cup half-and-half
- ¼ teaspoon black pepper
- 4 tomatoes, medium, sliced and roasted until tender
- 2oz. feta, crumbled
- 1 cup onions, thinly sliced
- ½ tablespoon butter
- ½ teaspoon fresh herbs – by your choice or fresh chopped rosemary

Directions:

1. Preheat oven to 350F and lightly grease 4 wide mouth Mason jars.
2. Beat together the eggs, salt, pepper and half-and-half.
3. Stir in tomatoes, feta, onions and fresh herbs.
4. Heat butter in small skillet and cook onions for 5-6 minutes or until tender; stir in egg mixture.
5. Transfer the mixture into Mason jars and transfer the jars onto baking sheet; bake for 35 minutes.
6. Allow quiche to cool for 5 minutes before serving.

Nutrition Facts

Serving Size 265 g

Amount Per Serving

Calories 218	Calories from Fat 133

	% Daily Value*
Total Fat 14.8g	23%
Saturated Fat 7.3g	36%
Cholesterol 273mg	91%
Sodium 571mg	24%
Potassium 474mg	14%
Total Carbohydrates 10.0g	3%
Dietary Fiber 2.2g	9%
Sugars 5.6g	
Protein 12.7g	

Vitamin A 31%	•	Vitamin C 32%
Calcium 16%	•	Iron 10%

Nutrition Grade B+

* Based on a 2000 calorie diet

Oven baked chili

Serves: 6

Time: 55 minutes

Ingredients:

- 1 cup salsa
- 1lb. ground beef
- 2 cups water
- 1 cup shredded Monterey Jack cheese
- 1 15oz. can black beans, drained and rinsed
- ½ tablespoon chili powder
- ¼ cup long grain rice
- ½ cup sliced green onions

Directions:

1. Preheat oven to 375F.
2. Brown beef in non-stick skillet and drain excess fat.
3. Add salsa, rice, water, beans and chili powder; stir to combine and bring to boil.
4. Spoon the mixture into six Mason jars and bake in preheated oven for 30 minutes.
5. Stir shredded cheese in each jar and bake further for 5 minutes.
6. Top with green onions before serving.

Nutrition Facts

Serving Size 304 g

Amount Per Serving

Calories 321	Calories from Fat 98

	% Daily Value*
Total Fat 10.9g	17%
Saturated Fat 5.4g	27%
Trans Fat 0.0g	
Cholesterol 84mg	28%
Sodium 683mg	28%
Potassium 755mg	22%
Total Carbohydrates 22.5g	7%
Dietary Fiber 4.5g	18%
Sugars 2.2g	
Protein 32.8g	

Vitamin A 11%	•	Vitamin C 5%
Calcium 20%	•	Iron 92%

Nutrition Grade B+

* Based on a 2000 calorie diet

Sweet potato with gorgonzola and eggs

Serves: 4

Time: 45 minutes

Ingredients:

- 1 sweet potato, large, peeled and cut in to ¾-inch cubes
- 3oz. gorgonzola cheese, shredded
- 1 small red onion, chopped
- 4 eggs
- 1 tablespoon olive oil
- Salt – to taste

Directions:

1. Preheat oven to 375F.
2. Toss sweet potato, onion and oil in large bowl; season with salt.
3. Transfer sweet potato and onion mixture into wide mouth Mason jars.
4. Roast the potatoes for 15 minutes; remove from the oven and crack one egg over each jar to top the potatoes. Sprinkle the eggs with gorgonzola cheese and bake further for 15-20 minutes.
5. Serve while still hot.

Nutrition Facts

Serving Size 115 g

Amount Per Serving

Calories 199	Calories from Fat 125
	% Daily Value*
Total Fat 13.9g	21%
Saturated Fat 5.9g	29%
Cholesterol 184mg	61%
Sodium 338mg	14%
Potassium 219mg	6%
Total Carbohydrates 9.2g	3%
Dietary Fiber 2.0g	8%
Sugars 2.9g	
Protein 11.0g	

Vitamin A 12%	•	Vitamin C 17%
Calcium 13%	•	Iron 10%

Nutrition Grade B-

* Based on a 2000 calorie diet

Stuffed bell peppers

Serves: 4

Time: 30 minutes

Ingredients:

- 4 red bell peppers
- 4oz. couscous
- 1 teaspoon lemon zest
- 1 tablespoon chopped coriander
- 4oz. mozzarella
- 3oz. tomatoes, chopped
- 1 small zucchini, finely diced
- 2 tablespoons basil, chopped
- 1 tablespoon butter
- 7fl.oz water, boiling
- Some olive oil

Directions:

1. Clean and seed the peppers and place in fitting Mason jar. Drizzle the peppers with some olive oil and broil, medium heat, for 5 minutes. Place aside.
2. Melt the butter in skillet; add zucchini and cook until golden.
3. Stir in couscous and cook for 1 minute. Add coriander and lemon zest and pour over the boiling water. Cover and place aside for 5minutes.
4. Stir in the tomatoes and basil and fill the peppers with this mixture. Top each pepper with mozzarella cheese.
5. Set the peppers under grill for 3 minutes or until the cheese is melted. Serve while still hot.

Nutrition Facts

Serving Size 233 g

Amount Per Serving

Calories 259	Calories from Fat 77

	% Daily Value*
Total Fat 8.6g	13%
Saturated Fat 4.9g	25%
Trans Fat 0.0g	
Cholesterol 23mg	8%
Sodium 204mg	9%
Potassium 433mg	12%
Total Carbohydrates 32.1g	11%
Dietary Fiber 4.6g	18%
Sugars 6.1g	
Protein 13.5g	

Vitamin A 87%	•	Vitamin C 268%
Calcium 23%	•	Iron 6%

Nutrition Grade B+

* Based on a 2000 calorie diet

Jalapeno cheddar muffins in jar

Serves: 2

Time: 30 minutes

Ingredients:

- 1 cup all-purpose flour
- ½ cup milk
- 1 egg
- ¼ tablespoon baking powder
- 1 tablespoon butter, melted
- ½ cup sharp cheddar cheese, grated
- ½ tablespoon pickled jalapeno, diced
- 2 tablespoons sour cream
- 1 tablespoon chives, fresh, chopped
- Salt – to taste

Directions:

1. Preheat oven to 375F.
2. In a small bowl whisk together all the dry ingredients, flour, baking powder and salt.
3. In separate bowl whisk milk with the egg and melted butter; fold wet ingredients in the dry ones and mix until almost smooth.
4. Stir in the shredded cheese and pickled jalapeno.
5. Divide the batter evenly between two Mason jars. Place the jars onto baking sheet and bake for 25-30 minutes.
6. Serve, topped with sour cream and chopped chives.

Nutrition Facts

Serving Size 196 g

Amount Per Serving

Calories 482	Calories from Fat 195

% Daily Value*

Total Fat 21.7g	33%
Saturated Fat 12.7g	64%
Cholesterol 137mg	46%
Sodium 285mg	12%
Potassium 372mg	11%
Total Carbohydrates 52.7g	18%
Dietary Fiber 1.8g	7%
Sugars 3.3g	
Protein 18.8g	

Vitamin A 14%	•	Vitamin C 2%
Calcium 40%	•	Iron 20%

Nutrition Grade B+

* Based on a 2000 calorie diet

Sushi in jar

Serves: 1

Time: 15 minutes

Ingredients:

- 1 Nori sheet, halved and cut into pieces
- ¾ cup rice, cooked
- ¼ cup carrots, shredded
- ¼ cucumber, seeded and shredded
- ½ avocado, medium, sliced
- Few slices pickled ginger
- 1 teaspoon rice wine

Directions:

1. Place half of Nori sheet in the bottom of a Mason jar.
2. Combine cooked rice with rice vinegar and place ¼ cup rice over Nori sheet.
3. Top rice with carrots and carrots again with ¼ cup rice.

4. Layer pickled ginger on top of carrots and top ginger with avocado slices.
5. Place remaining rice over avocado, top with cucumbers and final layer should be Nori sheet.
6. Serve after.

Nutrition Facts

Serving Size 348 g

Amount Per Serving

Calories 742	Calories from Fat 185

% Daily Value*

Total Fat 20.6g	32%
Saturated Fat 4.4g	22%
Trans Fat 0.0g	
Cholesterol 0mg	0%
Sodium 77mg	3%
Potassium 846mg	24%
Total Carbohydrates 127.3g	42%
Dietary Fiber 9.6g	38%
Sugars 4.6g	
Protein 12.5g	

Vitamin A 96%	•	Vitamin C 23%
Calcium 7%	•	Iron 38%

Nutrition Grade B+

* Based on a 2000 calorie diet

Risotto in a jar

Serves: 4

Time: 40 minutes

Ingredients:

- 8oz. mixed mushrooms, sliced
- 1 ¼ cup Arborio rice
- 1/3 cup white wine
- 3 cups stock, vegetable or chicken
- 1 cup broccoli, cut into florets
- ¼ cup grated parmesan
- 2 teaspoons olive oil
- 2 garlic cloves, minced
- 1 leek, medium, trimmed

Directions:

1. Preheat oven to 375F.
2. Heat olive oil in skillet; add leek and cook for 2 minutes over medium heat.
3. Add garlic and cook for 2 minutes more; add mushrooms and cook for 2-3 minutes or until tender.
4. Add rice and cook, stirring, until grains appear glassy.
5. Add wine and cook, stirring for 1 minute. Add stock and bring to boil; stirring occasionally.
6. Transfer the content into Mason jars; bake in preheated oven for 15 minutes.
7. Stir in broccoli and Parmesan cheese. Bake for 5-6 minutes more.
8. Serve after.

Nutrition Facts

Serving Size 288 g

Amount Per Serving

Calories 444	Calories from Fat 55

	% Daily Value*
Total Fat 6.2g	9%
Saturated Fat 1.3g	6%
Trans Fat 0.0g	
Cholesterol 81mg	27%
Sodium 87mg	4%
Potassium 559mg	16%
Total Carbohydrates 54.8g	18%
Dietary Fiber 3.2g	13%
Sugars 2.4g	
Protein 37.2g	

Vitamin A 11%	•	Vitamin C 42%
Calcium 5%	•	Iron 23%

Nutrition Grade B-

* Based on a 2000 calorie diet

Poha lunch jar

Serves: 4

Time: 15 minutes

Ingredients:

- 2 cups thick Poha
- ½ teaspoon cumin seeds
- 1 pinch mustard seeds
- 1 tablespoon oil
- 2 green chilies, chopped
- 2 curry leaves, chopped
- ½ tablespoon split black lentils
- 1 cup peas, cooked
- 1 cup carrots, shredded
- Hot water

Directions:

1. Heat oil in pan over medium heat; add mustard seed and cook until they crack.
2. Add lentils and once they turn golden add cumin seeds, green chilies and curry leaves.
3. Divide poha between jars and pour over prepared oil mix.
4. Mix well and add peas and carrots; pour over water, so it is ¼-inch above the level of poha.
5. Cover and let it rest for 10-12 minutes or until soft to the touch.
6. Serve and enjoy.

Nutrition Facts

Serving Size 118 g

Amount Per Serving

Calories 384	Calories from Fat 33

	% Daily Value*
Total Fat 3.7g	6%
Trans Fat 0.0g	
Cholesterol 0mg	0%
Sodium 32mg	1%
Potassium 191mg	5%
Total Carbohydrates 28.4g	9%
Dietary Fiber 7.7g	31%
Sugars 4.1g	
Protein 22.3g	

Vitamin A 100%	•	Vitamin C 27%	
Calcium 7%	•	Iron 7%	

Nutrition Grade B

* Based on a 2000 calorie diet

Ham and cheese roll ups

Serves 4

Time: 60 minutes

Ingredients:

- 8oz. sliced deli ham
- 1 cup mozzarella cheese, shredded
- 1 ball pizza dough
- Some mustard – to serve with

Directions:

1. Preheat oven to 400F.
2. Roll pizza dough to 12x8-inch rectangle.
3. Arrange ham slices over dough, leaving ½-inch edge free.
4. Sprinkle evenly with cheese and roll the dough, starting from the one of short ends.
5. Pinch seam together to seal and cut into slices that will fit into wide mouth Mason jar.
6. Bake in preheated oven for 45-50 minutes and serve while still warm, with some mustard.

Nutrition Facts

Serving Size 127 g

Amount Per Serving

Calories 284   Calories from Fat 99

	% Daily Value*
Total Fat 11.0g	17%
Saturated Fat 5.0g	25%
Trans Fat 0.0g	
Cholesterol 47mg	16%
Sodium 1051mg	44%
Potassium 163mg	5%
Total Carbohydrates 25.5g	9%
Dietary Fiber 2.2g	9%
Protein 21.1g	

Vitamin A 4%	•	Vitamin C 4%
Calcium 21%	•	Iron 11%

Nutrition Grade B+

* Based on a 2000 calorie diet

Stuffed peppers with egg

Serves: 2

Time: 10 minutes

Ingredients:

- 2 yellow bell peppers
- 2 tablespoons milk
- 2 eggs
- ¼ cup grated Parmesan
- Salt and pepper – to taste
- ¼ cup carrots, shredded

Directions:

1. Gently coat wide Mouth mason jars with some oil.
2. Cut the tops of peppers and remove the seeds and membrane. Place the peppers in the coated jars.
3. Whisk eggs and milk in a jug; season to taste and stir in the cheese and carrots.
4. Pour egg mixture into peppers and microwave for 3 minutes on low.
5. Remove and check the eggs; you can additionally microwave for 1 minute.
6. Serve after.

Nutrition Facts

Serving Size 209 g

Amount Per Serving

Calories 120	Calories from Fat 45

	% Daily Value*
Total Fat 5.0g	8%
Saturated Fat 1.6g	8%
Trans Fat 0.0g	
Cholesterol 165mg	55%
Sodium 95mg	4%
Potassium 416mg	12%
Total Carbohydrates 11.3g	4%
Dietary Fiber 3.2g	13%
Sugars 7.5g	
Protein 7.5g	

Vitamin A 181%	•	Vitamin C 256%	
Calcium 6%	•	Iron 8%	

Nutrition Grade A

* Based on a 2000 calorie diet

Mushrooms and chicken in creamy sauce

Serves: 2

Time: 15 minutes

Ingredients:

- 0.5lb. boneless chicken, cut into 1-inch pieces
- 10 mushrooms, quartered
- 5 peppercorns, crushed
- 2 teaspoons honey
- 2 tablespoons butter
- 2 spring onions, sliced
- 4 garlic cloves, minced
- ¾ cup tomato puree
- 1 ½ teaspoons Worcestershire sauce
- 1 tomato, diced
- ¼ teaspoon basil, dried
- Salt – to taste

Directions:

1. Divide the butter, spring onions, garlic and chicken between two Mason jars. Season with salt to taste.
2. Cover and microwave on high for 4 minutes; remove and add diced tomato, tomato puree, peppercorns, sauce and mushrooms.
3. Cover and microwave on high for 3 minutes. Add honey and basil, cover and microwave on high for 2 minutes.
4. Serve hot, garnished with spring onions.

Nutrition Facts

Serving Size 374 g

Amount Per Serving

Calories 417	Calories from Fat 185

% Daily Value*

Total Fat 20.5g	32%
Saturated Fat 9.6g	48%
Trans Fat 0.0g	
Cholesterol 131mg	44%
Sodium 257mg	11%
Potassium 1123mg	32%
Total Carbohydrates 22.4g	7%
Dietary Fiber 3.7g	15%
Sugars 13.8g	
Protein 38.3g	

Vitamin A 26%	•	Vitamin C 36%
Calcium 6%	•	Iron 34%

Nutrition Grade B+

* Based on a 2000 calorie diet

Eggplant special lunch

Serves: 2

Time: 35 minutes + inactive time

Ingredients:

- 1 eggplant
- ¼ cup ricotta cheese
- 2 tablespoons parmesan, grated
- ¼ cup mozzarella, torn into pieces
- ½ cup marinara sauce
- 1 tablespoon olive oil
- 1 garlic clove, minced
- 1 tablespoon extra-virgin olive oil
- ½ tablespoon basil, chopped
- Salt and pepper – to taste

Directions:

1. Preheat oven to 350F.
2. Combine parmesan and ricotta in a bowl.
3. Slice eggplant in ¼-inch thick slices and generously season with salt. Place in colander and set aside for 30 minutes.
4. Rinse eggplant and squeeze to remove excess liquid. Toss in a bowl with olive oil.
5. Combine marinara sauce with garlic in a jug and pour some of the marinara sauce in the bottom of a jar.
6. Begin layering lasagna, in two wide mouth Mason jars as follows; sauce, cheese mixture, eggplant, cheese mixture, sauce and then top with basil and mozzarella.
7. Bake the lasagna for 30 minutes; place on a wire rack to cool slightly before serving.

Nutrition Facts

Serving Size 354 g

Amount Per Serving

Calories 317   Calories from Fat 189

	% Daily Value*
Total Fat 21.0g	32%
Saturated Fat 5.5g	27%
Trans Fat 0.0g	
Cholesterol 18mg	6%
Sodium 385mg	16%
Potassium 769mg	22%
Total Carbohydrates 24.7g	8%
Dietary Fiber 9.8g	39%
Sugars 12.5g	
Protein 11.0g	

Vitamin A 11%	•	Vitamin C 11%
Calcium 22%	•	Iron 7%

Nutrition Grade B+

* Based on a 2000 calorie diet

Jar full of veggies

Serves: 1

Time: 30 minutes

Ingredients:

- ½ zucchini, medium, sliced
- ½ eggplant medium, sliced
- 1 tomato, medium, sliced
- ½ cup mozzarella cheese
- ¼ cup parmesan cheese
- 2 tablespoon bacon bits
- Salt and pepper – to taste
- 2 tablespoons breadcrumbs
- ½ cup marinara sauce

Directions:

1. Slice the veggies in ¼-inch thick rounds and season with salt and pepper.
2. Place one layer of eggplant, sprinkle with bread crumbs and top with one layer of mozzarella, tomato and zucchinis; repeat the layers until jars is full.
3. Pour over marinara sauce and gently move the ingredients in the jar so sauce can reach the bottom.
4. Sprinkle all with parmesan cheese and bake in preheated oven at 375F for 15-20 minutes.
5. Serve while still hot.

Nutrition Facts

Serving Size 355 g

Amount Per Serving

Calories 349	Calories from Fat 129

	% Daily Value*
Total Fat 14.4g	22%
Saturated Fat 7.1g	35%
Trans Fat 0.0g	
Cholesterol 33mg	11%
Sodium 964mg	40%
Potassium 825mg	24%
Total Carbohydrates 34.6g	12%
Dietary Fiber 5.7g	23%
Sugars 15.2g	
Protein 21.8g	

Vitamin A 34%	•	Vitamin C 46%
Calcium 47%	•	Iron 11%

Nutrition Grade A-

* Based on a 2000 calorie diet

Southwestern layered bell peppers

Serves: 2

Time: 30 minutes

Ingredients:

- 2 yellow bell peppers, tops removed, seeded
- ¼ teaspoon cumin
- ¼ teaspoon salt
- ¼ teaspoon pepper
- ½ teaspoon chili powder
- ½ cup can black beans, rinsed and drained
- 1 cup salsa, chunky
- ¾ cup instant brown rice
- ¼ cup corn, frozen

Directions:

1. Cut bell peppers in half and bake onto rimmed baking sheet in preheated oven for 15 minutes at 425F.
2. Meanwhile, boil ¾ cups water in a medium pot; stir in rice and return to boil.
3. Reduce heat to low and simmer for 5 minutes. Stir in corn, beans, salsa and mix gently.
4. Add cumin, salt, pepper and chili powder; place one pepper half in wide mouth Mason jar and top with ¼ prepared filling. Repeat the process with remaining filling and bell peppers.
5. Continue baking for 5 minutes and serve after.

Nutrition Facts

Serving Size 203 g

Amount Per Serving

Calories 205   Calories from Fat 14

	% Daily Value*
Total Fat 1.5g	2%
Trans Fat 0.0g	
Cholesterol 0mg	0%
Sodium 665mg	28%
Potassium 567mg	16%
Total Carbohydrates 42.7g	14%
Dietary Fiber 5.4g	22%
Sugars 5.1g	
Protein 6.3g	

Vitamin A 43%	•	Vitamin C 130%
Calcium 5%	•	Iron 13%

Nutrition Grade A

* Based on a 2000 calorie diet

38515889R00061

Made in the USA
Middletown, DE
19 December 2016